Aunt Bird

T0020891

Also by Yerra Sugarman

Forms of Gone

The Bag of Broken Glass

Aunt Bird

Yerra Sugarman

Four Way Books
Tribeca

For Feiga Maler

1919 – 1942

who died in the Kraków Ghetto

Library of Congress Cataloging-in-Publication Data

Names: Sugarman, Yerra, author.
Title: Aunt Bird / Yerra Sugarman.
Description: New York : Four Way Books, [2022]
Identifiers: LCCN 2021046021 | ISBN 9781954245143 (trade paperback) |
ISBN 9781954245228 (epub)
Subjects: LCGFT: Poetry.
Classification: LCC PR9199.4.S84 A85 2022 | DDC 811/.6--dc23
LC record available at https://lccn.loc.gov/2021046021

This book is manufactured in the United States of America and printed on
acid-free paper.

Four Way Books is a not-for-profit literary press. We are grateful for the assistance
we receive from individual donors, public arts agencies, and private foundations
including the NEA, NEA Cares, Literary Arts Emergency Fund, and the
New York State Council on the Arts, a state agency.

We are a proud member of the Community of Literary Magazines and Presses.

Contents

Loosened Inside Me

Tarnogród, Poland, 1939 / Houston, Texas, 2012

To Imagine No One Completely

Last Breeze Coming from a Jailed Girl's Body

(You have ghosts?)
(Of course I have ghosts.)
(What are your ghosts like?)
(They are on the insides of the lids of my eyes.)
(This is also where my ghosts reside.)
(You have ghosts?)
(Of course I have ghosts.)
(But you are a child.)
(I am not a child.)
(But you have not known love.)
(These are my ghosts, the spaces amid love.)

—Jonathan Safran Foer,
Everything Is Illuminated

[I have nothing to see her with]

I have nothing to see her with—
my aunt, whose life is a ripped page.

Does she suckle on wind,
forage among roots,
rummage near clawed feet,
drink handfuls of rain?

Aunt Bird

Once

Psalm
　　　　— to Feiga Maler (Aunt Bird)

When hate yells *kindness is forbidden,*
　　　　　　　　　geese lift themselves into flight
　　　　　　　　　　　　and hide behind clouds.
Once, war forced itself inside your body. Your raised arms
were antennae searching for the presence of God.

Now, I try to bring you back to life and harvest the words
　　　　　　　　　　on your tongue.
　　　　　　(Your speech was the language of wheat and barley.)

　　　　　　Prayers, you say, didn't move the soldiers
　　　　　　who hurled your name against the wall.

Tell me how to be a woman who revises this world
　　and makes food from light.

　　　　　　　　　*

It's 2020. The nation's shadow fans out and swallows a girl,
　　taken from her mother and father.

I admit, these days, I can hardly dip a spoon
　　into the sweetness of honey.
The girl is locked up in a cage with other girls. Lice spread

9

from the only comb they're permitted to share. She is called
Isabella G. To wash the black dirt from her face,
    she dampens a tissue with spit.

Razor wire slits the air. The nation stares.
                Please, teach me how to be a woman here.

                        *

I walk on ghosts, one time joyful in their skins. Like you,
    they trembled
                when they kissed their lovers' lips.
Learning to spell your name, I squeeze the letters with my hand
the way I would check a peach's ripeness.
                                You come alive.

                        *

Carry me on your back.
Braid us both into one candle.
Keep it bright inside walls of song.

Aunt Bird, Conjured

i.

When I still spoke the language of falling snow bending in the wind, and believed the world could be different—that we could learn to dress ourselves in the life of another— my young aunt's soul slipped into my bedroom and bloomed like a pear tree.

My fingers were beating a keyboard, dust zigzagging in the winter afternoon's woolen dullness. The river outside my window was taut along a horizon that clung to the fuzzy weave of sky. In that sky, the sun had begun to burn a hole, so that the atmosphere seemed to be fraying.

My aunt's sapling soul was nervous and mute, her mouth having been stopped up with earth for so long. Still, she grew—white flowers bursting from her chin—but remained silent.

ii.

Years later, haunted by my computer screen's membrane
of light, I discovered what her fate had been, her brief story
chronicled on the flare of the Internet's pages. But I couldn't
stop seeing her beyond the monitor's plastic skin.

(Genocidal little earth,
I imagined you sniffing
the hem of her skirt,

letting death piss
against her moon ribs

and carve up her nights, erase her desire
to inhabit a whole life,
to tear away her scrim of sadness.)

iii.

What I found out: she had taught in a school for girls and was killed in Kraków in 1942. She was just twenty-three. The Germans occupied the city, its vast squares stained by the dregs of each morning's milk-tea dawn.

On the far side of the Vistula River, the enemy had created a Jewish ghetto in the area known as Podgórze. Gone were the buzzing lanterns on the garrulous streets of Kazimierz, the quarter that had housed the largest Jewish population. And vanished from the porches and balconies, leaning on the breeze, were the slumping succahs, small shelters built in memory of the Jews who had lived in the desert, their roofs covered with fir tree branches.

No one could be seen praying on the riverbanks on the second day of the New Year anymore. No one could be seen tossing breadcrumbs into the water, the ritual for casting away sins. This was what the occupation authorities wanted. By March 20, 1941, the resettlement of the population was complete.

But after Passover, the ghetto began to look strange, carpenters and bricklayers building walls around it in the form of Jewish headstones. Large arches hunched along a crooked sky. Bars were fastened to windows, their boney shadows clutching crowded rooms.

iv.

(I share a skin with her now.

Her life unleashed
from time's body.

But how far can I picture
the edge of her breathing,

guess her collarbone's shape
or grasp a God gone wild?

I, who am so unencumbered,
watching the snow of a new January swarm

and soften my world with its fat whiteness.)

v.

Her life was like a thick soup in my mouth. Her name the
Yiddish word for "bird": *Feiga*. She wiped a grain of soil
from her lips, and I could hear the meat of her voice speak.
It climbed up and down my mind, so that she inhabited
the core of each thing.

Into the Shell of My Ear

Aunt Bird on What Happened to the Alphabet When the War Broke Out

The alphabet's letters, she whispered, quivered.
Each one fell on its belly as bombs shocked the air
and rattled needles on fir tree branches.

Every panicked letter, with nothing but the clothes
on its back, dove into the river's oily sinews.
The afternoon made of fever and stink.

Onto the bank, where weeds and thistles hissed,
she watched her neighbor, Joseph, haul a bloated *Lamed*,
burdock burrs stuck to its shirt, its face a bellows.

She saw a drowned *Vov* bob up-and-down as if it were tossing
in its sleep. It was tangled in wild lilac and mint,
buzzing clouds of flies above the writhing water.

That *Vov's* skin was wrinkled and blue.
One of its feet clung to a sock and the sole of a boot,
shattered pinecones in its hair —

[Bone by bone, she remembered]

Bone by bone, she remembered
what it was like to change from body into light,

that the month of March had had no time for grief
and tore up her belly
until there were just black plums there

like ancient letters split in two—
Al-ef, B-et, Gi-mel, Da-let.

She recalled she had once lived
blowing into a glass cup,

that the eyes and ears of the already dead
would sprout each night
from the city's starless womb.

And she dreamed, with elbows over tangled sheets,
of Limanowska, a curved eyebrow
of a ghetto street, paved with sighs,
sonorous with horseflies;

of the trolley on its hands and knees;

and of the Vistula's liquid muscles.

Kraków, she thought,
when the moon ate
its own stony light,

you watched me
in love only once,
how my stomach shivered.

She Lived Amid the Tumult of an Occupied City

The war thrust its hand inside her.
It churned her belly and her heart.
And she lived amid the tumult
of an occupied city—a donkey led

by its bridle. Surrounded by the enemy
laughing about the names it had for *Jew,*
she asked herself how many ways
she could say *madness* and watched

soldiers round up those whose fingers danced
on the words of the Torah.
Those who sat under a café's awning
stirring a cup of tea

were also rounded up; those bargaining
for beets piled high in the market;
those hanging wet sheets over balcony railings
were dragged from their apartments;

and those stopped to show identity cards
where peddlers sold bright balloons
were hauled away under the sharp beams
of streetlamps. Walls were peppered

with gunfire, bluebells speckled red.
Her people reeled along cobbled streets,
each person clutching a sack
containing things the enemy let them keep.

She was a short breath of a girl
who nursed an oriole
that sipped, in the mustard glow
of a Sabbath afternoon,

the crimson from poppies. A girl
who blamed herself for kissing
a boy beneath a tangerine moon
and for believing in anything

that didn't rust — resistance,
revolt, joy (sometimes) and songs
not exiled from the spirit.
To hell with the enemy, she trilled

in Yiddish, her nostrils widening,
her voice tugging the air. And for singing
she blamed herself also, scolded herself
in a language rising from her lips like steam.

[Night after night, what she saw in her sleep]

Night after night, what she saw in her sleep:
an upside-down *Havdalah* candle like the one she lit
to usher in a new week at the end of every Sabbath,

praying, "Blessed God, who separates light from dark..."

The candle in her dreams, like her real candle,
had four wicks and four braided strands of wax,
but produced no flames, only entrails of light.

And she dreamt God unhinged the constellations
and whisked away the stars. Uncreating. Uncreating.
The pitch darkness: a grave she couldn't find a way out of.

And she dreamt she was a stone a crow lifted
and tucked into the wind:
a girl born to memory that hushes the sun
and takes the place of trees' shadows.

When she woke, the war still raged
and the sky hardened into rock.

She wondered: why is God doing this?
And the thunder thundered: why are people doing this?

Despair swooping over her, her grief a kind of wingspan.

Delirious as the rain the river guzzled,
she became a stranger to herself,
circling her own shadow, searching for her beliefs,
her mind like shattered glass,

and the world stuck in her throat like a bone—

[The TV's on mute; its cool glow scrubs the room]

The TV's on mute; its cool glow scrubs the room. I'm at my computer, picturing my aunt with no suffering inside her, drinking milky coffee, and eating sponge cake under the striped awning of a Kraków café.

The 1938 city square gleams like a forehead. Nothing yet splits the voices from the streets. The rain of gunfire is still far away. Horse-drawn carriages rim sidewalks, bells stitched to reins clinking. The moment spreads out like the fingers of lamplight stroking shop windows. My aunt has many things to say, peeling the skin from her ideas.

Later, when time capsizes, she'll feel the hammer of loose heat the one summer she lives in the ghetto. She'll find herself at the bottom of each night's muck the only winter she survives there, her face the color of the plaster cracking on her ceiling.

She'll notice wind flatten the tall grass at Płaszów, the concentration camp on the outskirts of the city, and think about why violets strangely flourish along the camp's electric fence, or why young spruce trees spring up there, every needle a gravestone. *What's mourning?* she'll ask herself. *A mirror covered with a pillowcase flapping like a wing.*

26

During Wartime, Aunt Bird Reconsidered the Story of Abraham and Isaac

It was as if God lit a torch
in Isaac's throat, she said, in *Yitzhak's* gullet.
           Yitzhak: Hebrew for *laughter*.

His mouth contained a globe of the world,
a map of the sky, ashes and the Book of Life
where the names of those going to heaven are inscribed.

Was Abraham sickened
when God ordered him to sacrifice his son,

           ordered Abraham to listen
           as Isaac's sob bent the air
           into the sound the soul makes,

           commanded Abraham to split Isaac open
           and watch the blood run from his heart?

Was it for love or fear of God
that Abraham agreed to it, she wondered.

Abraham, who stood for *lovingkindness* —

           Did he pace the borders of himself

before tearing the yolk from his own spirit?

Was he asked to give in without understanding
like someone who can't read or write
signing a contract with a child's X and hands trembling?

Did Abraham let decency loose in the wind like feathers
from a pillow? Did he think God was the only truth?

Was noon glinting the way Abraham's knife did as he raised it
above his son, sunlight piercing him with its pins?

When God provided a ram instead,

      Abraham slid the blade down its neck
      to its tail, and Aunt Bird wondered,
      Will this son and father ever be happy again?

Once, she heard the pious soul
offers up joy because it belongs to God,
who always lets the soul retain it.

But how to hold onto joy if there was a torch lit
in Isaac's throat and God still stoked it?

Aunt Bird Opens the Steel Door of Gratitude

What was the country in her hand, but her own nation of
    wind-bent grasses?

What was she, but a body wrapped in its shroud of skin?

What was the world, but a flute her breath entered to play a song?

And she loved the flawed or damaged:
the prose of rambling thoughts
that came to nothing;
a cricket's shattered speech,
how it brought her solace;
ragged horizons torn by dusk; the sweating
plaster of her room in the ghetto.

Although she forgave the brutal beauty
of crocus petals sprayed with blood
on a neighboring street,
she hoped not one more flower
would bloom there again.

Every night, she stayed awake to warm the planets,
placing them in her armpits, the way she would warm a
    child's hands.

Every night, she scattered the names of the dead
in the breeze in her mind and hoped
someone would find the sound
of each letter there.

Of course, she prayed for miracles:

Stars, stars, don't fade away.
I'll give thanks for you again and again
because I live where green vines grow
over naked branches.

Because I live —

She imagined painting all the walls

in the world with a single rose
while she studied the salt light
of a Torah scroll, touching its parchment
with the small machine of one hand,
waving a green stem with the other.

If there must be walls, she thought,
let them be fragrant and made from prayers
whose vowels are the color of petals.

But she saw so much suffering
where walls stood — a rifle's shrill glare,
the pummeling of Yiddish words
until their guts stammered
and exploded like melons.

Would words return from the dead
without fear, she wondered, their groans
heard through teeth of the living?

Would they witness the enemy
grab an *Alef* by its throat
and hurl it against razor wire?
Would the words shriek as they watched

a soldier whirl a *Lamed* over his head?

So, she pictured herself
breaking down whole rooms, houses,
apartment buildings, streets, towns,

cities and entire borders,
liberating the bones underneath,
mending them, hoping
such beautiful ruin
would make each dead word sing.

[That her soul warmed itself in a body which would not persist]

That her soul warmed itself in a body which would not persist

That her heart flickered like a firefly inhaling and exhaling light

That the claws of each day tore away her skin bit by bit

That her dry tongue lapped the sky

That hunger lined her sentences with burlap

That her laughter turned into rubble

That crows whose wings scoured the clouds were like omens

That death was made from a syntax of bone and marrow

That she couldn't forget the translucent page of a face pocked
    with shrapnel

That grief clambered up and down her throat

That silence spoke

Once upon a time, after she had died

after, after she had died, her bones searched—by the rays of their own brightness—for the other dead of the ghetto. While they searched, they resembled miners wearing hard hats with lights. But her bones did not use a canary to warn them about danger because they knew that there had been enough death. How could there be more? They were sad as they kept searching, kept digging through earth. And only for this, they stayed bright.

One day, when morning was a pale blue handkerchief, her fingernails burrowed above the wet soil.

At night, it seemed that the deliverer-of-stars—the milkman's cousin—had tripped on a corner of darkness trailing from the roofs, his bucket spilling oleander-shaped lights above the city—still annexed by the enemy—so that the dry air started to weep stars and glisten.

She learned, after a while, to read the rain and windows that glowed persimmon in the spoiled meat of dusk.

Every evening, she watched the crooked seam of rooftops grow indistinct, shadowed in deepening grays as if a stick of charcoal had been pressed harder and harder on them.

34

She remembered that to her older sister, Chana, now also dead, the sky often looked unusually soft. Night unfurling itself above the imperfect horizon seemed to her a heavy wool blanket spread over God's interminable bed.

Chana would press her face against the windowpane and lick it to prove to herself that what was invisible was also real, as real as a knife that could snip, with one swift stroke, a poppy's flower.

Aunt Bird Recalls the Ladder of the Righteous She Observed During the War

Along the ladder of the righteous, on the rungs
between evil and good, a dusk of pigeons smeared the sky

and the language of joy was penniless, a vagrant.
God was a runaway child who ate the earth with a spoon

and licked the gooseflesh of our crowded room
so full our shadows couldn't lie down, standing

for weeks around a candle's nervous bird of light.
Along the ladder of the righteous, on the rungs

between evil and good, we threaded worry
through the eyes of needles. Chana rubbed

smuggled perfume on her wrists, the scent of poppies
even on her breath. Yakov printed letters of the alphabet

on his palm with a lump of coal and for each character
he remembered, he mouthed a gun's hollow boom.

Leah mistook stones for beans. She stirred them in a pot.
And we wondered if the sky would stop.

Along the ladder of the righteous, on the rungs
between evil and good, internees scratched their names

with their fingernails on detention center walls,
while customers on the city streets haggled for marzipan

and chocolate, dumplings and live geese, streets where
people dissolved like sugar cubes on the tongues of rain.

[Day's hem comes undone]

Day's hem comes undone above the high-rises circling my apartment building like prowling animals. The air is already lined with autumn rust. The city seems to ask me how I will bear myself in this infant light. Three hours of sleep slide behind my eyes as I look up, on the Internet, a Hebrew poem by Judah Halevi, imagining it might be something my Aunt Bird would have read in a book, underlining some of its phrases with a pencil. Maybe, as she turned the pages, she would gut her fears with the scalpel of a word.

[Before the city became rind and marrow]

Before the city became rind and marrow, my aunt was a
ribbon of daybreak.

—

Once upon a time, she hoped to split God's aloofness open
and tame it. But after the enemy invaded the land, she found
God's distance illegible: scribble on a page that a child
crumpled up and tossed into the famished air.

—

My aunt spoke a language with dirt under its fingernails:
Yiddish — its vocabulary composed of mourning and roots
ripped from the earth.

—

Living by the Torah's quartz light, she studied like a scholar —
like a man, they would have said back then. So she sobbed
imagining Hebrew letters lined up — *Chet, Tet, Yod, Kaf* — with
their faces pressed against a wall, gunfire shredding the
whimpering breeze.

—

Not even the executioners, who hunted the body and soul, could keep her from her longing which she anointed with honey, or from foraging a pitch dawn sky for clouds that would protect her passion and its rose-gold fire.

—

A wild boar wind lapped the maze of her ears, so she could hear her neighbors gulp back their fear, the churning froth of it.

—

And if her soul drowned, her body would be a boat made of willow tree branches: a delicate coracle keeling over in a frenzied sea.

—

Although it neglected her, she gave the world freshly-picked flowers.

[I'm always embracing her and discovering that one who is thin-boned can also be strong]

I'm always embracing her and discovering that one who is thin-boned can also be strong. What I know about my aunt, I learned from stories my mother told me, or from facts I gleaned when I crossed the bridge over the Vistula to see the Kraków Ghetto for myself. And, yes, there is the simple testimony I found on a website—her remains carried on the sea of a computer screen:

> *Feiga Maler was born in Kreshóv, Poland in 1919 to Anshel and Sheindl. She grew up in Tarnogród, Poland. She was a teacher and single. Prior to WWII she lived in Kraków. During the war she was in the Kraków Ghetto. Feiga was murdered in 1942 in the Shoah. This information is based on a Page of Testimony (displayed on left) submitted by her cousin.*

Source: DATABASE OF SHOAH VICTIMS' NAMES
Last Name: MALER
First Name: FEIGA
Father's First Name: ANSHEL
Mother's First Name: SHEINDL

Gender: Female
Date of Birth: 1919
Place of Birth: KRESHÓV, BILGORAJ, LUBLIN, POLAND
Marital Status: SINGLE
Permanent Place of Residence: KRAKÓW, POLAND
Profession: TEACHER
Place during the war: KRAKÓW GHETTO
Date of Death: 1942
Page of Testimony Submitter's Last Name: SHNITZER
Submitter's First Name: MALKA
Relationship to victim: COUSIN

—

A bookish young woman, words clung to her eyes. And every day was a day she might die. How did she learn to portion out light?

—

What was like honey caught fire more quickly.
What was a voice became a bowl of night.
What was destroyed is better left unsaid.

She Said, *Ours Were Bodies*

[She said, *Ours were bodies the world peeled*]

She said, *Ours were bodies the world peeled*
like grapefruits. Regarding the question of the Messiah's arrival—

she carried it in her pocket, where it dissolved
like the lapis tip of a star.

Mrs. Drobner, her neighbor, who had a beautiful dog,
scraped the air as if it were a fish,

always asking her what would happen to their people.
Winter cowered on my Aunt Bird's eyelids.

She wondered, *Was God's existence still possible?*
And tried to understand his silence (a stone on the bottom of
   a well).

Yiddish words were crushed like bones.
Yiddish—a language with wings one could stroke,

on which even sadness rose. Every day,
the thought of fresh bread she tried to tear

from the crust-colored clouds spilled
onto the floorboards of her mind. And she spoke with her friend,

Professor Steinberg, who considered the nothingness
they were born into, and believed he'd solved a mathematical
    problem

impossible even for Pythagoras. On the thin laps
of ghetto streets, along gutters' groins,

she corked her ears shut, but still overheard
the dead. She begged for miracles

with prayers parched as tulips drooping in a red-fat sun,
prayers that stung her more than the enemy's "Achtungs."

Why is news from the camps, she asked herself, *always wrong?*
And she missed streetlamps that astonished

sidewalks with flocks of shadows. And she longed
for the spoonsful of life she once ate with delight.

The dead, their hearts beating under pebbles

or inside clouds, visited regularly, she said.
They climbed up wild parsley
roots, or slid down the sky
on strings of rain.
  The living practiced lighting
the wick of the body,
although to live was not to stay,
but to burn toward grass and its silence,
or up behind a stammering star.

[Sometimes, the night held its breath]

Sometimes, the night held its breath
and she dreamt she returned to her mother's kitchen.

In her dream, a carp squirmed in the sink.

Her mother rolled up her sleeves,
then sharpened a knife, her arms thick bread loaves.

Blood spurted from the fish's belly, its sharp gills.

On the table, bones like combs.

The carp's stink jabbed the room.
The spit of onions cooking, sucking up grease.

Eat, she heard her mother command lighting a candle,
so that its flame shuddered
and its shine blushed in her blocky hands.

After she ate, she trimmed her lamp's wick
and curled up beside its brightness to read

a Hebrew poem by Shmuel HaNagid:

". . . and nobody speaks with understanding,
our souls dulled or dimmed . . ."

Words that slit her skin.

[Before the air gorged itself]

Before the air gorged itself
on fistfuls of lead,
wasn't she a girl who tore the sky
into pieces she tossed
like breadcrumbs?

Her fingers were brides
cooking jellied chicken and beet soup,
stitching leaves together to make a forest.

Trees burst into zebras.
Cabbages were witches.
She pressed her life to her lips and ate;
asked little of time galloping across fields,
whinnying at her window;

bore her stepfather's whip,
night sinking its claws
into the meat of dawn.

She was a girl who watched a moth
fly like a reconnaissance plane
zigzagging across the moon,
a moth on a crooked journey

toward some uncertain knowledge,

a hunger inside each singed wing.

[She felt neither joy nor its salt-white absence]

She felt neither joy nor its salt-white absence

and didn't know how to see it, the life she'd been flung into,
so that she was like a blind person tapping her cane on obstacles.

Along thin-skinned streets, she prayed,
although when she pictured God, she saw
the short, hairy legs of a fly.

Once, she thought the dead entered her room
like flakes in a slanted snowfall,
their cries creaking hinges.

But what could their cries do?

[A voice can be like flesh]

A voice can be like flesh, lit by the brightness of its wounds.

—

And if she'd been a well, she'd be abandoned by her own water.

—

What the world scrawled on the palms of her hands was
    never legible.

—

The upside-down city around her made a sound severed from
    its echo.

—

And God was the mayhem in the wind.

[When she was fenced off even from herself]

When she was fenced off even from herself,
she had that strangled feeling as if the alphabet forgot her lips.

How did she mend thoughts that snapped like strained violin
    strings?
Sometimes, her mind was a turnip she buried in the ground.

Licked by wind, old chairs were left scattered on her ghetto street,
abandoned by Jews rounded up for transport.

But to where?
And she watched grief sit on the shoulders of women

whose legs were knitting-needle thin,
women who covered their eyes with their hands

and still recited blessings over candles lit to honor the Sabbath.
Once, she overheard someone say, "My heart was a sparrow—

now it's caught in a vice." Reading Dostoevsky, she was shocked
to learn he spent four whole years in a Siberian prison

with only the Bible as his friend. This gave her hope, so she
    could still fall in love

with a certain kind of star bright as a glowing *złoty*, a shiny coin

in the sky, even when she thought the moon was inside out.
Soldering bits of life together like scraps of steel, she and her
    sister Chana

believed it would be a sin to ever laugh again. But, they laughed,
    Lord,
they laughed and their hearts were brown wings.

[Aunt Bird said she had to heave herself from sleep]

Aunt Bird said she had to heave herself from sleep
to study how the wind's blade whisked the air,

that she wanted to grasp the reckless motion of being —
its spit and grime and ruin —

because nothing expired completely
except time eating its own body.

She taught me I was made out of crumbling
and to bring into the open the damaged

heart of even my self-willed dark,
although fear sprouted from my skin

and my voice was a wing flapping wildly.

Loosened Inside Me

[I wanted Aunt Bird always loosened inside me]

I wanted Aunt Bird always loosened inside me.
I wanted her to grind coffee's bitter beans
and toss salt over my room's shoulder.

I wanted to clip her fingernails
and wash behind her ears, words
rushing from her mouth like clouds carried by wind.

I wanted to see the roots and ledges
of what was boarded up in her mind,
the slopes of her thighs and her slack belly.

I wanted her to hitch our nights to a cart
in which we would sit at the brink of breaking
and she would stroke my head and sing.

I wanted to dress her in her breathing.

[For who is she]

For who is she
to the contraption of history,

to the damaged engines of the world?
Who is she to my river sweating mist?

And who is she to you,
Lord-who-does-not-salvage,

God-of-bombardments
from whom I'm weaned?

[And may there be no more needles]

And may there be no more needles
of rain in her words.

No more moon-blade shucking
her eyes' blue irises.

No one trying to ambush her.
The war's nights no longer patrolling her nights —

their nerves no longer severed at the root.
May the guttering dusk not suck away her days.

May she not fall over the earth's bloody rim.
May her absence not wander with itinerant shadows,

her sadness not coo like a mourning dove.
Let me see the woven basket of her fingers,

how they shave away the world's silence.
Let lamentation keep me

from forgetfulness —
its frail and mortal body.

**[*See*, I say to Aunt Bird, *what a sturdy
house your soul makes*]**

See, I say to Aunt Bird, *what a sturdy house your soul makes
not letting history dissolve like mentholated pills on our tongues.*

The day's undisturbed fabric hangs from my window,
the pane exposing tobacco-stained light,
its ravishing impermanence and volley of dust.

Bless that light's rubber band strain
and boney groin.
How it bronzes my room.

Bless the slender stalk of Aunt Bird's body,
the pins her tears become.

[Sometimes Aunt Bird asks, *What tethers me to this world?*]

Sometimes Aunt Bird asks, *What tethers me to this world?*
What's my past that's tangled in wind?

Was I a foreigner in a house of foreigners,
an edge along what was already all margin?

O, her eyes singe my newspapers, burn them
into quills of steam in the sun's fickle beams,

the refugee alphabet imprinting itself on air.
Aunt Bird's fingers serve all that is milk-bright.

I wake up and hope I can hold such luster inside me,
lift it to my mouth and eat.

Tarnogród, Poland, 1939 /
Houston, Texas, 2012

[It is just before the war cracks the land open like an egg]

It is just before the war cracks the land open like an egg.
Her mother's voice—rooted in the naked grief of the Jews—

gives the kitchen walls goosebumps,
describing bones of fear that glow

like spectacles perched on a stern schoolteacher's nose.
Vertebrae shudder against ribs

so stressed, they slit flesh and skin.
Jaws stiffen into ache that causes hush and hunger.

Her life is a solitude of sweaty palms shrugged off
by the earth: clammy hands stroking the sky's sunken belly.

And it seems that even sparrows roost on telephone wires
that are nerves in the air,

that even the Vistula flows only when swaddled like a newborn
in the tight-lipped moon's cool light.

But she studies every fine hair on her forearms to learn
there is still an abundance of world

and pretends she is waltzing pressed to the bosom
of a different time when she could replace panic with song.

Lord, she would sing, *my longing is a hungry toddler tasting each
    new toy.*
This she knows: the breakable body has an undertow

and she moves forward like a pony wearing blinders,
seeing only the smallest sliver of things.

[An owl's hoot scoops the pulpy dark]

An owl's hoot scoops the pulpy dark.

I'm waiting for morning to be honed
into shrill bands, for flaps of daybreak
and for the air crammed with rain to soothe itself.

I'm waiting for the world to glide through me,
chew away its umbilical cord
and disconnect me from this pail of blue-black night.

Sometimes, there is a fever and want's rind in me.
Sometimes, there are questions eased only by sleep.
Sometimes, I'm an amnesiac whose mind is nailed shut

even as I take apart the sky,
even as I dismantle wind,
even as I pry history open.

I curl up beside longing's wilted petals,
shapes of words stitched to my lips,
syllables constructing candid sentences
that memory refuses to admit.

[Aunt Bird moves to Kraków before the bombardments and before the sky]

Aunt Bird moves to Kraków before the bombardments and
    before the sky
is pulled back like a bandage from the skin,

before Germans storm Poland in September 1939
and she understands how she has grown away from herself,

so that in the basin of her belly
there is a scalpel moon trying to cut away the familiar stars.

She writes her name in dirt when she leaves her village for the
    shiny city.
She takes her house's pulse,
a house whose every throb she knows,
believing her past will fall away.

She strokes her mother's cheek.

She doesn't yet understand what plays the strings of her desire.

I try to fill in
the holes in her story,
the many hollows.

What is her life and its small engine
I want to summon up with a pen,
describe from a pool of silence,
define with muscles of grief?

[Slowly, the air is cured of its dark calluses]

Slowly, the air is cured of its dark calluses;
there are splinters now
of unimpeachable, fractured brightness.

Nothing along this horizon speaks to me,
not the swallows witnessing an oak root meander
as they perch and throng on sloping rooftops.

I lose faith in how I summon up Aunt Bird
through the sift of self,
by draining the muddy Texas bayous

and by swallowing rooms that have not been sealed,
in which seventy years weigh less
than the words I use to write these poems.

[Light howls and history peels its own skin]

Light howls and history peels its own skin.
I imagine trains bombarded in 1939. They unfurl their whines
and lumber backwards. I picture my aunt navigating

the spokes of Kraków streets
where bruised leaves spin. She wants stillness.
She wants to brush her face against the earth,

places from which the souls of the dead spring.
When fear echoes through her,
she prays for silence or sleep

or begs for mercy from the ordinary:
the threading of a needle.
She knows something will always drag to the ground

the chambers of her body.
But she still believes in living
with every breath's rise and fall.

[Language can bear the everyday grace of slumber]

Language can bear the everyday grace of slumber,
the white knuckles of my fist,
my mere body as elastic — mine, but not mine

like the familiar bleats a hawk makes that evaporate quickly.
This morning, rain stitches the wind.
I gaze at the sky's impoverished, tin-ceiling light

and feel amnesia's weightlessness
counter what dark I carry.
I claw my mind that huddles next to spiderwebs elsewhere.

Vestiges of memory: apertures in time, coin-shaped.
The homeless hours are nomads, though rich as woodgrain
to we who are a kind of havoc.

[We who are a kind of havoc]

We who are a kind of havoc,
living beneath the scarred lungs of clouds —

we inhale smoldering air, yelling *oxygen!*
We dispatch sorrow, crying *enough!*

In the dark kernel of her day, my aunt straightens
the rumpled blanket on her bed.

Along floorboards, she charts a trail to her past,
to her students' sinewy chatter.

The froth of their laughter tingles her throat.
Their muscular voices hoist her to the ceiling. She is suspended.

If only she could stay there.
She remembers her mother's singing and her belly relaxes.

Ballads rise from her calmed gut
in a place that always lurches and hisses.

She pictures herself unfastening the chain around the ghetto's
    neck,
rubbing a pummeled sky — pretending it is the back of a sick child.

She imagines shaking out her street like a fresh sheet she
    could rest on
without listening for footsteps, dogged and booming.

But she knows better than to dream herself again
sipping happiness like a root drinking water.

[My hands are talons that claw my life among these words]

My hands are talons that claw my life among these words,
syllables growing fat on scraps of memory
springing back and forth like branches in wind.

My aunt knows wreckage is a bond
we have until we are dust
settled on the floor of sleep.

I'm learning a human cry can be made flesh,
that to remember is both plague and song.
And I consider this:

the world continues to spin;
human lives find hope in movement,
in the gaping mouth of time.

[All morning, I am just my body]

All morning, I am just my body.

A dove's sob dents the wind,
but bears witness to no one's history.
It is only the cry of something common,
the small sum of a lung at home in the homeless breeze.

The bright suburban air swells, unloosening its reek.

I wanted, once, to see through things, to look inside them
and find the sequestered glow of their sweet grief.

Now, I just touch what I see: the clock's fluorescent numbers
stamped on my kitchen's stiff dark;
knives clinging to a magnetic strip above the sink;
feathers stuck to a cracked sidewalk.

And the copper flower nodding its consent
amid the trash and weeds, how do its petals survive
with such delicate skin?

Stupid sorrow. Your affliction is glass. How easily we are broken.

Even the sun's amenable light today turns its back on my window.

How can I keep from falling?

[Simone Weil wrote about force]

Simone Weil wrote about force
that it converts both slave and master into stone.

"It is the x that turns anybody who is subjected to it into a *thing*."

"Exercised to the limit," she noted, "it turns man into a thing
in the most literal sense: it makes a corpse out of him."

After she said this, after she let hunger consume the flesh
from the armature of her bones,
the Nazis began to call their Jewish victims "objects."

And I worry that the pain force inflicts is fruitless —
that it's all for nothing —
like trying to nail a shadow to a wall.

Am I wrong to believe in redemption
when there are events that scorn us,
that fill our mouths with snow
and coat our tongues with silence?

At twilight, I try to measure the sky,
the incommensurate, hibiscus-red sky

and look for a voice that looks for its throat.

[who knows how light works]

i.

who knows how light works

one window streaked with poppy

the other hammered tin

glint of a knife stuck in winter

the sometimes crumbling sky

and she living in her brevity

the world breaking on her tongue

she spits it up again

so small the prayers

that sway the earth in her

ii.

the past she stores in a raft in her mind

a stepfather whose face eats the air

his whip crooning

her nest of worry

sucking on her room's onion glow

but to what end

the war taking what she might not see again

sky tangled in a tree

pencil-lines of bark

this ghetto by the river's sinews

sighs springing from her mouth

slap like water

against the gorge of night

iii.

the birch stump soothed by snow

a requiem on the radio shucks the streets' rot

signs advertising jewelry cleansed of blood

this interrupted body — hers and not

a small machine that won't give solace

will not grieve in oily moonlight

courage is like meat packed in ice

the air jumbled with crows

it can't free anything

iv.

she washes herself

in her mother's name

folds its syllables

inhales memory

her mother's hands like lakes

seeping through her eyes

v.

to forget desire

shining its gaudy brightness

the labor of the body

a small collapsing house

she could walk for days

threading dirty streets

toward her own vanishing

we are simple animals

safe for awhile

not like she was

wishing for stillness

away from inescapable eyes

prey for another

To Imagine No One Completely

[Tonight, the moon is scarred, an aperture in the mist]

Tonight, the moon is scarred, an aperture in the mist.

The wind, all harrow and spleen, is a violence spilling. It pummels still-bare pear trees, the docile brownstones and a bodega's flimsy fruit-stands lit by hooked streetlamps. Their radiance amplifies the fragility and impermanence of all things.

Even this late, motorcycles barrel down the avenue, unzipping silence, grinding air.

Time hisses.

Fog shorn from the sky's torso.

I'm learning to hold my world close, as I would a frightened child.

How will my life, already ripe, play out? This is something I can ask myself because I have the luxury to ask. Nothing in my room responds, not the tousled sheets, not the books heaped on my desk, not the pen and its bed of shadow, not my hands' complex machinery.

My fear of dying scorches my insides. It swells within me so I feel I'll give birth to a terror I'm not fit to resist, a darkness that leaks into my eyes. Blinded by it, I sense how everything is lined with its own vanishing.

We stay alive and hope nothing bad will happen, but death will happen. It's the seeming impossibility that breathes through us. If we're lucky, those who care about us and are obligated to us will be present when our soul seeps from the boundaries of our skin.

Someone bending over us will run their hand tenderly through our hair. In their other hand, they'll hold a wedge of darkness, grief undoing them. As they lean beside what is most real, they'll wrestle with a body that no longer belongs to the one they love.

But to whom does this emptied container of the body belong?

* * *

Without having the departed's corpse to mourn, can the living ever stop grieving?

Writing about the ancient Greeks, Robert Pogue Harrison observes, "To deprive the grief-stricken of the loved one's remains was a calamity worse than the one that brought on their grief, for it denied them the means by which to meet their obligation."

He also notes, "[T]he torments suffered by the souls of the unburied in Hades are imaginary projections of the torments and guilt suffered by their loved ones under the sun."

The vacated vessel of the body — its soul unloosened and released — is ordinarily bequeathed to those who lament and weep. What, then, is more heartrending than to have no body to bury and honor through ritual, so that we can unchain our misery and "humanize" the earth?

This is a chapter in my aunt's story, she who was cleaved from the pitted ground too early.

What happened to her body is unknown.

"The work of getting the dead to die in us, as opposed to dying with our dead" is formidable, even hopeless, "when the dead body goes missing," says Harrison. He also recalls mourning without the deceased's remains is so wretched "that some ten days after Hector's death Troy is on the brink of disaster."

My mother was separated from my aunt during the war. After it ended, thinking about her dead sister, my mother spent hours each day tugging her cheeks and rocking back and forth in a kitchen chair. It was to her that my aunt's corpse belonged, though it was never found.

My brother and I inscribed my aunt's history, quickly fading, on the back of my mother's tombstone, although an epitaph alone cannot pierce this desolation:

not knowing where the basin of light that was her body now exists.

[silence pares my lips]

silence pares my lips

night kneading daybreak

doeskin of a childless dawn

clouds pacing like caged animals

I mourn again my wrong belief

that evil can ignite the arrival of good

mourning that becomes an alleyway

to prayers flown like flags

lowered to half-staff

to a satin grieving

I study the language of her bones

somewhere they are singing

the dirge of my aunt's missing body

but where does her body reside

her death stumbling through me

[To imagine no one completely vanishes]

To imagine no one completely vanishes is to believe a person does not endure only as a body. Then what continues to live beyond the regions of the flesh? Memory, its salt and honey in our mouths. But how do we feel if we can't honor the remains of a loved one who's passed? How do we carry on?

What I can't write: her life as it was precisely inscribed on the earth.

What I write: my debt to her and my guilt—she who belonged to this world where I wash my hands and face and rub my eyes to see her more clearly.

Does my aunt consign herself to me as rain falls on rain and a man in a red jacket hammers at brick on the roof across from mine? Do I hammer at her life in vain with my imprudent words because I have no exact archive of her body?

Inside me is the history of a shadow lining my porous throat, clinging to my tongue. Here, where I live, dust falls gently on my books—dust which is simply skin.

Harrison says that a person can "die in spirit" if they do not bury the people they love. He cites the moment in *The Iliad* when Achilles "withholds the body of the slain Hector" from his father, King Priam:

"Dung lay thick on the head and neck of the aged man for he had been rolling in it, he had gathered and smeared it on with his hands."

How did my mother bear the weight of not burying her sister's body, the distress of not knowing how my aunt's life ceased? My mother, who never swallowed any peace, cradled her unresolved sorrow in her mind and heart.

She was a drum. The darkness striking her made a muffled sound that echoed throughout our split-level, suburban house, which was meant to shelter her from the ubiquitous eyes of her grief. But there were few serene hours in our home.

My mother believed in God, but of what use was God to her?

[a tumult of birdsong]

a tumult of birdsong

mourning coats each thing

with the iris of affliction

sky smeared with bleach

the dense smell of a mouse dead somewhere in my room

its severed body

for which I shine a flashlight in every corner

and discover only a dust ball's gray fur

unremitting experience circles us from birth to death

arguing that courage is contrived

and even if we want to shun it

when experience is taken from us

there is not even the purple of a thistle

permitting us the means

to grow within

the world's body and its ravishing infidelities

Last Breeze Coming from
a Jailed Girl's Body

Kiddush

—to Feiga Maler (Aunt Bird)

In this world, tyrants gaze at themselves in mirrors
and comb their hair. Withered leaves fall out
stabbed by spikes of sunlight. Commands claw the air.

In this world, where there are still celebrations, the last breeze
coming from a jailed girl's body,
      the final breath released
            from the lungs of a seven-year-old—
            she is called Jakelin C—

floats past barbed wire nettles budding on a fence
that surrounds a detention camp for migrants: knife-lit
            human invention.

In this world, I touch a glass with my mouth
and drink to all creation.

        Tell me how I can keep from falling,
        how to turn grief into a green stem sprouting

           so it is not just a stem, but joy.

Notes

The poems in *Aunt Bird* were inspired by the brief life of one of my mother's sisters: my Aunt Feiga Maler, whom I never met. In this book, I reimagine her experiences during World War II and the Holocaust. Before the outbreak of the war, she moved from a shtetl — a small Jewish town in Poland — to the Polish city of Kraków, where she died at the hands of the Nazis in 1942 in the Kraków Ghetto. Another sister, my Aunt Chana Maler, the eldest of my mother's three sisters, was also murdered by the Nazis in the same ghetto during the Holocaust.

The Kraków Ghetto was created by the Nazis during World War II in German-occupied Poland. Such ghettos were among the more than 44,000 camps and incarceration sites established by Nazi Germany and its allies, who used these places for a range of purposes: forced labor, detention of people thought to be enemies of the state, and for mass murder.

To systematically execute millions of people, the Nazi regime set up imprisonment facilities and killing centers in Germany and in the territories it conquered. Concentration camps, death camps, forced-labor camps, transit camps, ghettos, and other sites of persecution and state-supported murder, were also used as part of the Nazi regime's mass extermination of European Jews. During World War II and the Holocaust, the genocide of European Jews was one of the

Third Reich's primary goals. The Holocaust was the planned murder and oppression of six million Jews by the Nazis, the Nazis' allies and collaborators.

Like many survivors of the Holocaust — of the Shoah, as it is called in Hebrew — my parents were reticent about revealing their experiences during World War II, and about the Nazi extermination of our family members; what little I do know about my Aunt Feiga, I learned from my mother: Pearl Maler Sugarman, who died in Toronto, Canada in 2000 at the age of eighty. My mother spoke to me about her murdered sisters in fragmentary, intermittent memories. I hope that the poems in this book reflect this fragmentary discourse, which I inherited.

Specific information about my aunts' final years I discovered fortuitously by means of random Internet searches. In 2006, one search brought to light a Page of Testimony in the Central Database of Shoah Victims' Names at Yad Vashem — The World Holocaust Remembrance Center. This Testimony was provided by our cousin: Malka Anshel Shnitzer, who reported my Aunt Feiga's place and year of birth as Krzeszów, Poland, 1919. In 2020, I came across another document on the Internet in the Holocaust Survivors and Victims Database of the United States Holocaust Memorial Museum. This second document is among a "grouping [which] contains registration forms completed by the Jewish inhabitants of Kraków, Poland, in 1940 and coordinated by the Jüdische Gemeinde in Krakau (Jewish

Community in Kraków) in response to a Nazi order."

This document records my Aunt Feiga's birthplace as Tarnogród, Poland, and her birthday as "12 Sep 1915." I decided to state her year of birth as 1919 in accordance with what I initially learned from Malka's Testimony, and in keeping with the information I provided in poems from this book that I had already published in literary journals. Malka's Testimony also declares that Feiga was a teacher "murdered in the Shoah."

My aunt's name, Feiga, comes from the Yiddish word *feygele* (פֿייגעלע), which means "little bird," and is the diminutive of *foygl* (פֿויגל), the word for "bird."

In *Aunt Bird*, there are references to the Yiddish and Hebrew languages, which are different. The Yiddish writing system makes use of Yiddish spellings and Hebrew script. Yiddish is also sometimes transliterated, replacing the Hebrew script with the Roman script. Yiddish (ייִדיש) — born of exile and Diaspora — is usually considered a West Germanic language that contains Hebrew, Aramaic, as well as elements from Slavic and Romance languages. Until the Holocaust and the Nazis' annihilation of six million European Jews, Yiddish was the everyday language of eleven to thirteen million Jewish people worldwide. In the early 20th century, it was becoming a major Eastern European language, and in the US, it was the principal language in Jewish immigrant communities.

Until the eve of the Holocaust, Yiddish literature, theater, and cinema, flourished. In the US, Jewish writers and poets created from it an important, new, and genuinely American literary establishment, second only to the English one.

The Holocaust caused a decline in the use of Yiddish, as the European Jewish communities that spoke the language were mostly destroyed. Today, there are approximately three million Yiddish speakers worldwide. It is the first and majority language of Hasidic and Haredi communities.

To verify details and facts about life in the Kraków Ghetto, and for inspiration and for information, I consulted with these two texts: *The Cracow Ghetto Pharmacy* written by Tadeusz Pankiewicz, and translated from the Polish by Henry Tilles; *The Girl in the Red Coat: A Memoir* written by Roma Ligocka with Iris Von Finckenstein, and translated by Margot Bettauer Dembo.

This book's opening epigraph is from the novel *Everything Is Illuminated* by Jonathan Safran Foer, Mariner Books edition, 2015.

Parts of "Psalm" and "Kiddush" take information from a variety of newspaper articles about children interned in migrant camps in the US along the Mexican border.

In the poetic sequence "Aunt Bird, Conjured," some of the details about the city of Kraków and the Kraków Ghetto are based on information from Tadeusz Pankiewicz's *The Cracow Ghetto Pharmacy*.

In "Aunt Bird on What Happened to the Alphabet When the War Broke Out," the letters of the alphabet referred to are Yiddish letters transliterated from Hebrew to Roman script.

In "[Bone by bone, she remembered]," the "ancient letters" referenced are Hebrew letters.

The Jewish religious ceremony *Havdalah* mentioned in "[Night after night, what she saw in her sleep]," marks the end of the Sabbath, and the ushering in of a new week.

The poem "During Wartime, Aunt Bird Reconsidered the Story of Abraham and Isaac" refers to the binding of Isaac—the Akedah—as recounted in Genesis 22 in the Hebrew Bible.

The information about my Aunt Feiga Maler provided in "[I'm always embracing her and discovering that one who is thin-boned can also be strong]" is based on Testimony given by my cousin Malka Anshel Shnitzer located in the Central Database of Shoah Victims' Names at Yad Vashem – The World Holocaust Remembrance Center.

In "[Sometimes, the night held its breath]," the quote from the Hebrew poem by Shmuel HaNagid is my interpretation of

Peter Cole's translation of HaNagid's poem "On Fleeing His City." Cole's translation reads, "…and not a one speaks wisely, / their souls blunted, or blurred."

"[Simone Weil wrote about force]" quotes from and considers Weil's 1940 essay, "The Iliad, or the Poem of Force," which she wrote after the Fall of France and the German invasion of France during World War II.

"[Tonight, the Moon is scarred, an aperture in the mist]" and "[To imagine no one completely vanishes]" quote from and discuss the book *The Dominion of the Dead* by Robert Pogue Harrison, The University of Chicago Press, 2003.

Acknowledgments

I am grateful to the editors and staff of the following publications in which work has appeared, sometimes in different versions: *Arts & Letters*, *Bat City Review*, *Cherry Tree*, *Colorado Review*, *Image*, *New Orleans Review*, *Ploughshares*, *The Los Angeles Review*, and *Tupelo Quarterly*.

Thank you to the students in the Department of English Language and Literature at the University of Toledo in Ohio, and to their professor, the poet Timothy Geiger, who produced my chapbook *From Her Lips Like Steam* (Aureole Press at The University of Toledo, 2019). The following poems from the chapbook reappear in *Aunt Bird*, often in varying forms: "Aunt Bird, Conjured," "Aunt Bird on What Happened to the Alphabet When the War Broke Out," "She Lived Amid the Tumult of an Occupied City," "During Wartime, Aunt Bird Reconsidered the Story of Abraham and Isaac," "Aunt Bird Opens the Steel Door of Gratitude," "She imagined painting all the walls," and "[That her soul warmed itself in a body which would not persist]."

My infinite gratitude goes to Martha Rhodes, my editor, and my friend, for her remarkable insights about *Aunt Bird*, and for seeing so much more than I could see.

My thanks to my entire Four Way family for making this book happen: Martha Rhodes, Ryan Murphy, Sally Ball, Clarissa Long, Bridget Bell, and Hannah Matheson. Thank you also to Owen Lewis for his enthusiasm, and for going the extra mile.

I am also grateful to the National Endowment for the Arts, and to the Canada Council for the Arts for their support.

For giving me time to write and think and grow, thank you to the University of Houston's Doctoral Creative Writing Program, and to its Department of English. Thank you, as well, to the MFA Program for Writers at Warren Wilson College, where this manuscript began to take shape.

I would like to thank the following people for their support and guidance: Karen Brennan, Jehanne Dubrow (without whom this book would not have come to be — thank you for your love, brilliance, and vision), Jamie H. Ferguson, Joanna Fuhrman, Malachi Hacohen, the late Tony Hoagland, James L. Kastely, Wayne Koestenbaum, Boni Joi, Pamela Lischin, Sharon Mesmer, David Mikics, Ange Mlinko, Alicia Suskin Ostriker, Jean-Paul Pecqueur, Kevin Prufer, Jason Schneiderman, Grace Schulman, Martha Serpas, Stephanie Strickland, and Alan Williamson.

My love and gratitude to my family for their amazing support, and especially to my brother Alan Sugarman, who, along with my late parents, have made my writing life possible.

Yerra Sugarman is also the author of *Forms of Gone* (Sheep Meadow Press, 2002), which won PEN American Center's PEN/Joyce Osterweil Award for Poetry, and *The Bag of Broken Glass* (Sheep Meadow Press, 2008), poems from which received a National Endowment for the Arts Fellowship. Her other honors include a Glenna Luschei *Prairie Schooner* Award, a Canada Council for the Arts Grant for Creative Writers, the Poetry Society of America's George Bogin Memorial Award and Cecil Hemley Memorial Award, a Chicago Literary Award, and a "Discovery"/*The Nation* Poetry Award. Her poems have appeared or are forthcoming in *Ploughshares*, *Colorado Review*, *The Nation*, *AGNI*, *Prairie Schooner*, *New England Review* and elsewhere. She earned an MFA in Visual Art from Columbia University, and a PhD in Creative Writing and Literature from the University of Houston. Born in Toronto, she lives in New York City.

Publication of this book was made possible by grants and donations. We are also grateful to those individuals who participated in our 2021 Build a Book Program. They are:

Anonymous (16), Maggie Anderson, Susan Kay Anderson, Kristina Andersson, Kate Angus, Kathy Aponick, Sarah Audsley, Jean Ball, Sally Ball, Clayre Benzadón, Greg Blaine, Laurel Blossom, Adam Bohannon, Betsy Bonner, Lee Briccetti, Joan Bright, Jane Martha Brox, Susan Buttenwieser, Anthony Cappo, Carla and Steven Carlson, Paul and Brandy Carlson, Renee Carlson, Alice Christian, Karen Rhodes Clarke, Mari Coates, Jane Cooper, Ellen Cosgrove, Peter Coyote, Robin Davidson, Kwame Dawes, Michael Anna de Armas, Brian Komei Dempster, Renko and Stuart Dempster, Matthew DeNichilo, Rosalynde Vas Dias, Kent Dixon, Patrick Donnelly, Lynn Emanuel, Blas Falconer, Elliot Figman, Jennifer Franklin, Helen Fremont and Donna Thagard, Gabriel Fried, John Gallaher, Reginald Gibbons, Jason Gifford, Jean and Jay Glassman, Dorothy Tapper Goldman, Sarah Gorham and Jeffrey Skinner, Lauri Grossman, Julia Guez, Sarah Gund, Naomi Guttman and Jonathan Mead, Kimiko Hahn, Mary Stewart Hammond, Beth Harrison, Jeffrey Harrison, Melanie S. Hatter, Tom Healy and Fred Hochberg, K.T. Herr, Karen Hildebrand, Joel Hinman, Deming Holleran, Lillian Howan, Thomas and Autumn Howard, Catherine Hoyser, Elizabeth Jackson, Jessica Jacobs and Nickole Brown, Christopher Johanson, Jen Just, Maeve Kinkead, Alexandra Knox, Lindsay and John Landes, Suzanne Langlois, Laura Lauth, Sydney Lea, David Lee and Jamila Trindle, Rodney Terich Leonard, Jen Levitt, Howard Levy, Owen Lewis, Matthew Lippman, Jennifer Litt, Karen Llagas, Sara London and Dean Albarelli, Clarissa Long, James Longenbach, Cynthia Lowen, Ralph and Mary Ann Lowen, Ricardo Maldonado, Myra Malkin, Jacquelyn Malone, Carrie Mar, Kathleen McCoy, Ellen McCulloch-Lovell, Lupe Mendez, David Miller, Josephine Miller, Nicki Moore, Guna Mundheim, Matthew Murphy and Maura Rockcastle, Michael and

Nancy Murphy, Myra Natter, Jay Baron Nicorvo, Ashley Nissler,
Kimberly Nunes, Rebecca and Daniel Okrent, Robert Oldshue and
Nina Calabresi, Kathleen Ossip, Judith Pacht,
Cathy McArthur Palermo, Marcia and Chris Pelletiere,
Sam Perkins, Susan Peters and Morgan Driscoll, Patrick Phillips,
Robert Pinsky, Megan Pinto, Connie Post, Kyle Potvin,
Grace Prasad, Kevin Prufer, Alicia Jo Rabins, Anna Duke Reach,
Victoria Redel, Martha Rhodes, Paula Rhodes, Louise Riemer,
Sarah Santner, Amy Schiffman, Peter and Jill Schireson, Roni and
Richard Schotter, James and Nancy Shalek, Soraya Shalforoosh,
Peggy Shinner, Anita Soos, Donna Spruijt-Metz, Ann F. Stanford,
Arlene Stang, Page Hill Starzinger, Marina Stuart,
Yerra Sugarman, Marjorie and Lew Tesser, Eleanor Thomas,
Tom Thompson and Miranda Field, James Tjoa,
Ellen Bryant Voigt, Connie Voisine, Moira Walsh,
Ellen Dore Watson, Calvin Wei, John Wender, Eleanor Wilner,
Mary Wolf, and Pamela and Kelly Yenser.